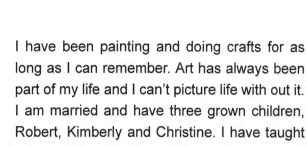

Blossoms and Bows

by Sherry Payne

I have been painting and doing crafts for as long as I can remember. Art has always been part of my life and I can't picture life with out it. I am married and have three grown children, Robert, Kimberly and Christine. I have taught and have at different times had a retail store. My passion is flowers and I love to paint them. I have been painting for over 40 years and have been in many shows and exhibits. I am pretty much self-taught taking every class I can with any teacher I can. It isn't so much the finished project as what you can learn from that project and that teacher. I once had a teacher tell me that all the beauty and patterns in the world are in nature and we can enjoy them if we take the time to look. How right you are Bill. Bill Powell, you are a very wise man. Thank you for teaching me to take the time to look and enjoy.

Thank you, the reader, for buying this book and I hope I can share my joy of painting with you.

Dedication

This book is dedicated to all those who love to paint and on a personal note to Maria for her constant encouragement, to Ellie for being the friend in need, to my family for their good wishes and support, and to the Lord above, without who all this would not be possible.

Disclaimer: The information in this book is presented in good faith. No warranty is given to the user relating to the material used in this book. Since we have no control over the physical conditions surrounding the application of the information contained herein, Sherry Payne will not be liable for any untoward results, or charges made against the user for claims of patent or copyright infringement.

Would you like to meet people who share the same love of painting as you?
Become a member of The Society of Decorative Painters. For more information write:
The Society of Decorative Painters
393 N. McLean Blvd. • Wichita, • KS 67203-5968

Distributed by: 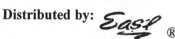 ®
Essential Authors Services Ltd.
P.O. Box 22088 • St. Louis, MO • 63126
Phone: (314) 892-9222 • Fax: (314)892-9607
Visit our web site at: http:\\www.easlpublications.com

Project Index

Miscellaneous Supplies:

Pattern	Tracing paper
Water container	Graphite paper white and grey
Stylus	Reusable palette paper
Pencil	Magic eraser
Krylon 18K Gold pen	Sandpaper different grades
Gold leaf glue	Gold Leaf (Composition)
Baby wipes	Brush cleaner
Tack cloth	Wood fill
Liquid Nails	Tissue paper
Two rubber bands	13 small wood apple halves
2 medium pear halves	Three wood leaves 1"
Bee's wax	Delta Gel Medium
Iron	Pressing cloth
Freezer paper	Heat transfer pencil

Velvet sticky back paper from Cache Junction
Delta Stencil -Etruscan #952060018
Delta Renascence foil adhesive and Mother of Pearl foil
Delta Monogram Magic letter stencils
Tiny square piece of balsa wood dowel cut into 4 pieces ¼" long
Delta Textile Medium
Eberhardfaber easy-pen #878201
Painters tape (blue) two different widths 1" and ½"
Sponges - sea sponge and a make-up sponge

Brushes:

I use all Daler Rowney Expressions brushes. What ever your brush preference make sure you use the best you can afford. There is a difference. Always use the largest brush you can handle. The larger the brush the smoother the float. You can also maximize floats by adding Delta Color Float to your water.
E85 pointed round #4, #2, #6
E60 flat shader #4, #8, #20
E57 angle shader ½"
E67 filbert #4b, #6, #8
E51 liner #10/0, #1
E52 oval mop # ¼" ¾"
2" flat glaze brush

Paint:

The paint I use is Delta Ceramcoat

Autumn Brown 2055	Black 2506
Black Cherry 02484	Butter Yellow 02102
Chambray Blue 02514	Charcoal 02436
Chocolate Cherry 02538	Dizzel Grey 02452
Dusty Plumb 2456	Fleshtone Base 2082
English Yew Green 02095	Green sea 02445
Lavender Lace 2016	Light Ivory 2401
Magnolia White 02487	Mallard Green 02491
Navy Blue 2089	Payne's Grey 2512
Purple 2015	Rose Cloud 02450
Rose Petal Pink 02521	Sweetheart Blush 02130
Village Green 02447	White 2505
Wild Rose 02485	

Gleams

Kim Gold 02602	Aqua Cool Pearl 2614
Baby Blue Pearl 2609	Pinkie Pearl 2612
Violet Pearl 2623	Silver 2603

Delta Sparkle Glaze
Delta Crackle
Delta Surface Cleaner and Conditioner

General Directions:

Surface Prep: All surfaces have holes and imperfections, fill and sand smooth, wipe with a tack cloth. Sealing the wood is your own personal preference. Some people do, some don't. To seal, simply apply one coat of Delta's wood sealer. The end product will reflect the care you take now.

Wash: Mix 4 parts water with 1 part paint. This mix is used to glaze over the surface to change or highlight a color.

Tracing patterns: If you are like me, my finished piece doesn't always match the original pattern. But that's ok. Painting is not an exact science. It is suppose to be fun. I trace my patterns on the computer by scanning them or coping them onto velum. This gives you a pattern that will last a long time. If you do not have access to a computer or copy machine you can still trace the pattern onto velum in ink to produce a more durable pattern. When transferring your pattern to your surface it is only necessary to trace the outside lines onto your work. After the base coating is finished you can then trace other lines as needed.

Smoke Surface: Using a candle, secure it in a holder or stand, hold a spoon over the flame until the candle smokes. This smoke is what you want on your piece. Holding a spoon over the flame until it smokes, carefully turn your piece above the smoke to capture the smoke on the surface. Keep turning your piece until the desired effect is obtained.

Tissue Paper surface: Scrunch up tissue paper into a ball. Pull apart and tear into small pieces. Apply to the surface with paint. Don't brush out the creases and folds but leave them in for texture.

Finishing: When finishing a piece I am usually in hurry but don't be. This step is just as important to the overall look of the piece. If it is a piece that will be used a lot I use Minwax Poly-crylic finish. If it is for decoration I use Delta varnish. You can use the finish you like.

6

Credits

Paint:

Delta Technical Coatings, Inc.
2550 Pellissier Place
Whittier Cal, 90601
http://deltacrafts.com
800-423-4135

Brushes:

Daler Rowney/ Robert Simmons
2 Corporate Drive
Cranberry, NJ
609-655-5252

Wood Items:

Rose Box 29L and Basket 55c
Recycle Box 11
Bentwood, Inc
PO Box 1876
170 Big Star Drive
Thomasville, GA 31799
912-226-1223

Popcorn Box, Signboard, Candles
Viking Woodcrafts, Inc.
1317 8 St SE
Waseca, Minnesota 56093
507-835-8043

Basket 773203
Kit Stoner
Painter's Paradise
111 Parish Lane
Wilmington, De 19810
302-478-7619

Crafters Porta Palette
PO Box 161
Clarksboro, NJ 08020
Port-a-palette@prodigy.net
877-224-9665

Signboard, lamp
Artist Club
P.O. Box 8930
Vancouver, WA 98668-8930
1-800-845-6507
http://Artistsclub.com

Windchime
S&G, Inc.
Po Box 805
Howell, MI 48844
517-546-9240

All glass products
B&B Etching Products, Inc.
18700N. 107th Ave Suite 13
Sun City, AZ 85373

Tin tray
Barb Watson's Brushwork's
20600 Avenida Hacienda
Riverside Ca 92508-2425

Apples, pears, gingerbread people,
butterflies, dragonflies, charms,
leaves
Bear with Us Inc.
3007 S. Kendall Ave
Independence, MO 64055

Gold leaf foil
Houston Art
10770 Moss Ridge Road
Houston, TX 77043-1175

Initial Box, Mirror, clock base
Walnut Hollow Farms, Inc.
1409 State Road 23
Dodgeville, WI 53533

Reusable palette paper
Wingate Packaging, Inc.
Cincinnati, Ohio 45241
http://wingatepacking.com

18K Gold Leaf Pen
Krylon
Sherwin-Williams Diversified Brands
Inc
Solon OH 44139
1-800-4-Krylon

Linens
Wimpole Street Creations
Barrett House
PO Box 540585
North Salt Lake, UT 84054-0585
801-299-0700

Doll Kit Heirlooms from the Heart
18" porcelain doll kit.
Bell Ceramics
PO Box 120127
Claremont Fl 34712-0217
352-394-2174, 1-800-874-9025

Velvet sticky back paper
Cache Junction Seitec Inc.
1717 South 450 West
Logan Ut 84321
800-333-3279

Rose Box
color photo on front cover

Palette:

Black Cherry	Chocolate Cherry
Green Sea	English Yew Green
Village Green	Lt. Ivory
Magnolia White	Kim Gold
Rose Petal Pink	Wild Rose
Butter Yellow	Sweetheart Blush
Mallard Green	Charcoal
Chambray Blue	White
Rose Cloud	Dizzel Grey

Gold leaf   Sponge
Stencil

Instructions
Filbert or large flat brush
1. Paint the box sides with two coats of Black Cherry. The first coat can be applied with water to keep it smooth.
2. To the top and bottom, apply two coats of Chocolate Cherry. Let dry.

Sea sponge
3. To the sides, sponge on Kim Gold and Chocolate Cherry. Keep the colors softly blending as you sponge; you only want a hint of Kim Gold to show.

Graphite paper and tracing paper
4. Transfer your pattern to the top of the box.

Small filbert or small round brush
5. Base coat the ribbon and the dogwood with Light Ivory, the leaves and dogwood centers with Green Sea, the tulips with Rose Petal Pink, and the roses with Wild Rose.

The Leaves
Angle shader or flat
1. Shade with English Yew Green.
2. Highlight with Village Green.
3. Tip the leaves with Sweetheart Blush.

Liner or script liner brush
4. Put in the vein lines with Village Green.

Small filbert
5. Pick out several leaves and wash them with Mallard Green to add variety to the leaves.

Angle shader or flat
6. Side load with Charcoal and shade the extremely dark areas.
7. Side load with Village Green and re-enforce the extremely light areas.

Dogwood:
Angle shader or flat
1. Shade petals with Village Green.

Liner
2. Add vein lines with Village Green

Angle shader or flat
3. Highlight with Magnolia White.
4. Shade dark areas with Chambray Blue
5. Re-enforce light areas with White
6. Tip ends with Sweetheart Blush
7. Shade dark areas with Sweetheart Blush

Dogwood Centers
Angle shader or flat
1. Shade with English Yew Green
2. Highlight with Village Green and add a sparkle with White.

Roses
Angle shader or flat
1. Load with Rose Cloud and tip into Rose Petal Pink. Run your brush back and forth on the palette to get a nice blending of color.
2. Starting with the back petals, paint in the roses. With each petal pick up more and more Rose Petal Pink. Blend the color on the brush before you paint each petal. Paint the rose petal by petal not row by row. The petals should get lighter as they come forward.
3. When the rose is complete go back and shade with Wild Rose
4. 2nd shading-Shade extremely dark areas with Sweetheart Blush.
5. Highlight with Magnolia White.
6. The extremely light areas are reinforced with White

Stylus
7. Add dots to the center with Magnolia White.

Tulips
Liner or script liner brush
1. Add vein lines with Magnolia White.

Angle shader or flat brush
2. Shade veins with Village Green

Angle shader or flat
3. Shade the tulips with Rose Cloud
4. Highlight the tulips with White
5. Add deeper shading to the petals with Chocolate Cherry

Ribbon
Angle shader or flat brush
1. Shade with Drizzle Grey
2. Highlight with Magnolia White
3. 2nd shading to the ribbon is with Chambray Blue.
4. Mix Chambray Blue with Chocolate Cherry and shade the extremely dark areas of the ribbon. (two parts cb one part cc)
5. Highlight with White.
6. Side load an angle shader with White.

8

7. With the heel of the brush next to the ribbon wiggle on the ruffle. Pay attention to the way the ribbon turns.
Stylus
8. Add White dots
Glue pen
9. Add stripes along the edge of the ribbon with the glue pen.
10. When the glue dries press on the Gold leaf.
11. Brush off excess.
12. Wipe off box top with a tack cloth.

Box Bottom
1. Measure up 2" from the bottom and tape around the box.
Filbert brush
2. Paint the box below the tape with Chocolate Cherry. Let dry.
Make up sponge
3. Position the stencil along the bottom edge of the box and tape in place.
4. Using the gold leaf glue and a small makeup sponge, sponge glue through the stencil around the bottom of the box. When you pick up the glue on the sponge blot off on a paper towel before you sponge onto the surface.
5. Continue around the bottom of the box.
6. Let dry, then press the gold leaf onto the glue. Wipe off excess.
7. Apply glue to the studs let dry

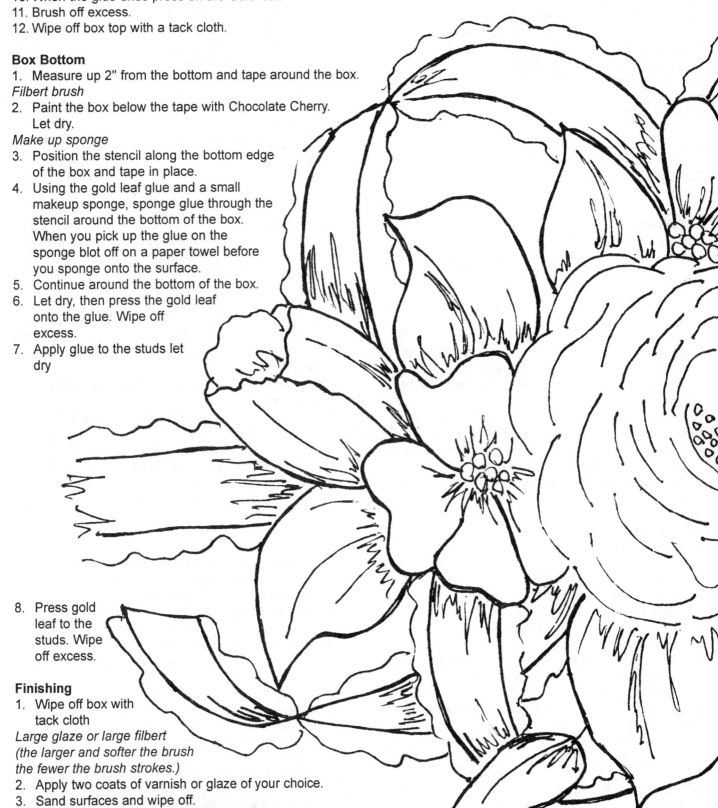

8. Press gold leaf to the studs. Wipe off excess.

Finishing
1. Wipe off box with tack cloth
Large glaze or large filbert
(the larger and softer the brush the fewer the brush strokes.)
2. Apply two coats of varnish or glaze of your choice.
3. Sand surfaces and wipe off.
4. Apply one more coat of varnish or glaze.
5. Wax with bee's wax.
6. Apply velvet paper to the inside of the box.

connect with pattern at bottom of page

connect with pattern at top of page

©Bayne

Rose Lamp

color photo on front cover

Palette:

Rose Cloud

White

Black Cherry

Village Green

English Yew Green

Gold Leaf

Tissue Paper

Base and Light

1. Base coat with Black Cherry

2. Paint on pieces of tissue paper with Black Cherry. Let dry.

3. Dry brush the surface with glue.

4. Press on Gold Foil. Brush off excess.

5. Finish as described in the front of the book.

Flowers

1. Flowers are base coated with Rose Cloud.

2. Highlight with White on the tips.

3. Leaves are done with a double loaded brush of Village Green and English Yew Green. Press down and pull up.

4. The line work and stems are done with a dirty Green brush.

Rose Mirror

color photo on inside front cover

Palette

Light Ivory

White

Green Sea

Village Green

Rose Petal Pink

Payne's Grey

Sweetheart Blush

Wild Rose

Chocolate Cherry

Rose Cloud

English Yew Green

Magnolia White

Chambray Blue

Mallard Green

Charcoal

Black

Renaissance Foil Mother of Pearl

Gold Leaf

Instructions

1. Basecoat the front with Light Ivory, the edge with Chocolate Cherry and the back with Rose Cloud.

2. Dip the sponge in water and wring out. Wipe the front with the damp sponge. Sponge the front with Magnolia White, Rose Petal Pink and Rose Cloud. Keep it light. Colors should blend together softly and not be blotchy.

Butterfly

1. Base coat the butterfly with Chambray Blue and shade with Payne's Grey. Let dry.

Leaves

1. Base coat the leaves with Green Sea.

2. Shade with English Yew Green.

3. Highlight with Village Green.

4. Tip the leaves with Sweetheart Blush.

5. Put in the vein lines with Village Green.

6. Pick out several leaves and wash them with Mallard Green to add variety to the leaves.

7. Side load an angle shader with Charcoal and shade the extremely dark areas.

8. Side load with Village Green and re-enforce the extremely light areas.

Roses

1. Base coat the area of the rose with Wild Rose

2. Load a flat shader with Rose Cloud and tip into Rose Petal Pink. Pull your brush back and forth on the palette to get a nice blending of color.

3. Paint in rose petals. With each row of petals pick up more and more Rose Petal Pink the petals should get lighter as they come forward.

4. Shade with Wild Rose

5. Shade the extremely dark areas with Sweetheart Blush.

6. Highlight the light areas with Magnolia White.

7. Add dots to the center with Magnolia White.

Butterfly

1. Apply adhesive to the butterfly wings. Brush out and apply two light smooth coats. (Adhesive can be thinned with water.) Let dry

2. Apply foil.
3. Outline the butterfly wings with Black
4. Add dots with a stylus.
5. Glue on to frame with Liquid Nails

Finishing
1. Paint comma strokes around the edges with adhesive and a round brush.
2. Press gold leaf
3. Brush off excess and wipe with a tack cloth.

Rose Basket
color photo on inside front cover

Palette

Black Cherry
Rose Petal Pink
Rose Cloud
Green Sea
Mallard Green
Kim Gold
Magnolia White

Light Ivory
Wild Rose
English Yew Green
Village Green
Sweetheart Blush
Charcoal

Satin Glaze
¼ yd fabric

Instructions

1. Pick out a small piece of fabric and cut to desired size and shape. Iron out all wrinkles.
2. Base coat the top with two coats of Light Ivory.
3. Place the fabric on the wet paint and smooth into place.
4. Apply a heavy coat of Satin Varnish to the fabric. Let dry.
5. Sand the fabric lightly and wipe off any particles.
6. Sponge on Green Sea and Village Green to the area around the fabric.
7. Draw on circles where roses will be and base coat the leaves with Sea Green.
8. Paint a band of Kim Gold around the remaining edge of the fabric.
9. Paint intersecting lines to the area around the fabric with Kim Gold.
10. Lightly (load sponge and blot, then apply) sponge Light Ivory on the area around the fabric to mute the gold lines. Blending as you work.

Leaves

1. Shade with English Yew Green.
2. Highlight with Village Green.
3. Put in the vein lines with Village Green.
4. Pick out several leaves and wash them with Mallard Green to add variety to the leaves.
5. Side load an angle shader with Charcoal and shade the extremely dark areas.
6. Side load with Village Green and re-enforce the extremely light areas.
7. Tip the edges with Sweetheart Blush.

Roses

1. Load a flat shader with Rose Cloud and tip into Rose Petal

Pink. Run your brush back and forth on the palette to get a nice blending of color.
2. Paint in roses. With each row of petals pick up more and more Rose Petal Pink. The petals should get lighter as they come forward.
3. Shade with Wild Rose
4. Shade extremely dark areas with Sweetheart Blush.
5. Highlight with Magnolia White.
6. Add dots to the center with Magnolia White.

Finishing

1. Paint the edge with Kim Gold.

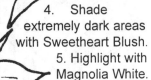

Dogwood Clock

color photo on page 26 • pattern on following page

Palette

Magnolia White	English Yew Green
Village Green	Green Sea
Chambray Blue	Mallard Green
White	Navy Blue
Dusty Plumb	Autumn Brown
Trail Tan	

Gold Leaf
CD

Instructions

1. Base coat the surface with English Yew Green. Let dry and apply a second coat if needed.
2. Base coat the edge with Magnolia White. Let dry and apply a second coat if needed.
3. Using a candle smoke the surface.
4. Using the glue pen draw a line around the edge of the clock.
5. Press gold leaf onto the glue areas. Wipe off excess.
6. Glue a CD to the center of the surface. Drill a hole in the center and insert clock parts.
7. Add hands as instructed
8. Trace on flower pattern.

Dogwood

1. Basecoat the petals with Magnolia White.
2. Shade petals with Village Green.
3. Add vein lines with Village Green
4. Highlight with White.
5. Shade dark areas with Chambray Blue

6. Re-enforce light areas with White
7. Tip ends with Dusty Plumb.
8. Shade dark areas with Navy Blue.

Dogwood Centers

1. Base coat with Green Sea
2. Shade with English Yew Green
3. Highlight with Village Green and add a sparkle with White.

Branch

1. Double load a round brush in Autumn Brown and Trail Tan.
2. Paint in branches.

Leaves

1. Base coat the leaves with Green Sea.
2. Shade with English Yew Green.
3. Highlight with Village Green.
4. Tip the leaves with Dusty Plumb.
5. Put in the vein lines with Village Green.
6. Pick out several leaves and wash them with Mallard Green to add variety to the leaves.
7. Side load an angle shader with Navy Blue and shade the extremely dark areas.
8. Side load with Magnolia White and re-enforce the extremely light areas.

Finishing

1. Apply a hook to the back and hang.

Initial Box

color photo on page 26

Palette

English Yew Green	Black
Kim Gold	
Tape	Tissue paper
Gel Medium	

Instructions

1. Apply two coats of English Yew Green to the box.
1. Tape off a stripe on the top of the box and one around the edge of the box.
2. Crumple up a piece of tissue paper then tear into small pieces. You will be painting the tissue paper on to the box. Do not try to smooth out bumps but leave them in. Place a small piece of tissue paper onto the box, with Green Sea paint the tissue adher-ing it to the box. Continue this procedure covering the outside of the box.
3. Antique the box with a mix of equal parts of gel medium and Black. Apply to surface and wipe off.
4. Sponge on Kim Gold. Let dry.
5. Take off the tape and paint the stripes with Black. Let dry.
6. Tape stripes on the black and paint the area with English Yew Green.
7. Take off tape and paint initials with Kim Gold.
8. Paint the inside of the box with English Yew Green.

Finishing

1. Cut a piece of velvet paper to fit the bottom inside of the box and stick down.

Clock

Payne

Recycle Box

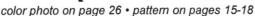

color photo on page 26 • pattern on pages 15-18

Palette

Autumn Brown	Trail Tan
Fleshtone Base	Butter Yellow
Dusty Plumb	White
Payne's Grey	Green Sea
English Yew Green	Village Green
Rose Petal Pink	Black Cherry
Magnolia White	Black

Instructions
1. Base coat the bottom with Magnolia White and the top with Black Cherry.
2. Smoke the bottom.
3. Trace on the pattern.

Apples
1. Paint all the apples with Black Cherry
2. Highlight with Butter Yellow

Pears
1. Base coat with Fleshtone Base
2. Apply Autumn Brown to the roof.
3. Outline shingles with Payne's Grey
4. Sign and hole are painted with Payne's Grey
5. Stipple on flowers with English Yew Green, Village Green, Black Cherry, and White.

Leaves
1. Base coat with Green Sea
2. Shade with English Yew Green
3. Highlight with Village Green Tip with Dusty Plumb
4. Add vein lines with Village Green.

Branch
1. Double load a round brush with Autumn Brown and Trail Tan and paint in the branch

Flowers
1. Base coat with Rose Petal Pink
2. Highlight with White
3. Shade with Dusty Plumb

Centers
1. Stipple in with Butter Yellow
2. Shade with Autumn Brown
3. Highlight with White
4. Add black and white dots with a stylus

Glue on all the apples and pears as indicated. (if you want to hang this piece don't glue the pieces on the back)
Finish as indicated in the front of the book.

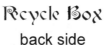

Recycle Box
back side

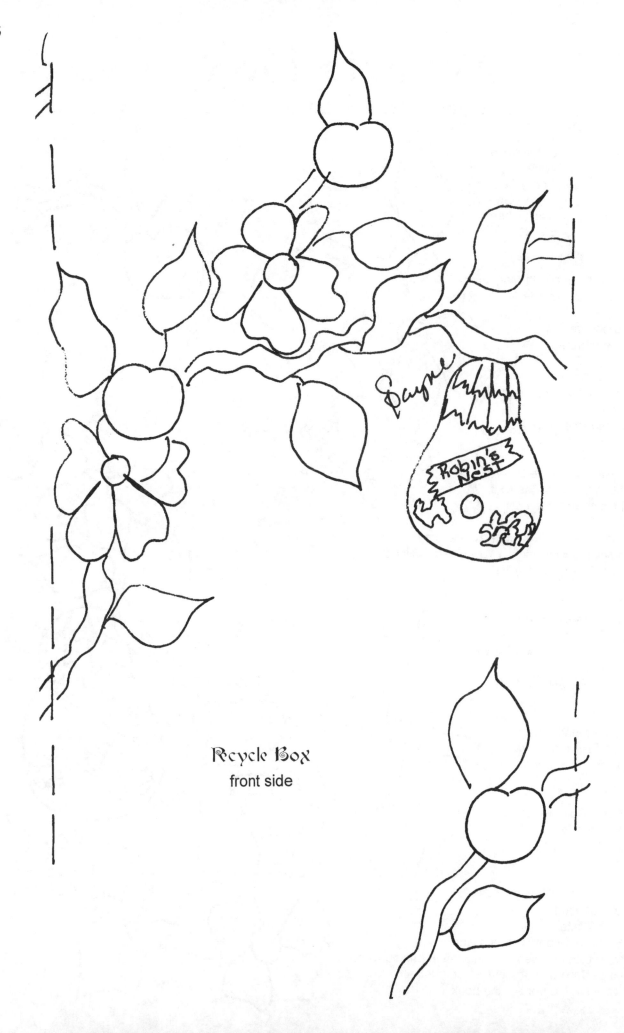

Recycle Box
front side

Recycle Box
right side

Recycle Box
left side

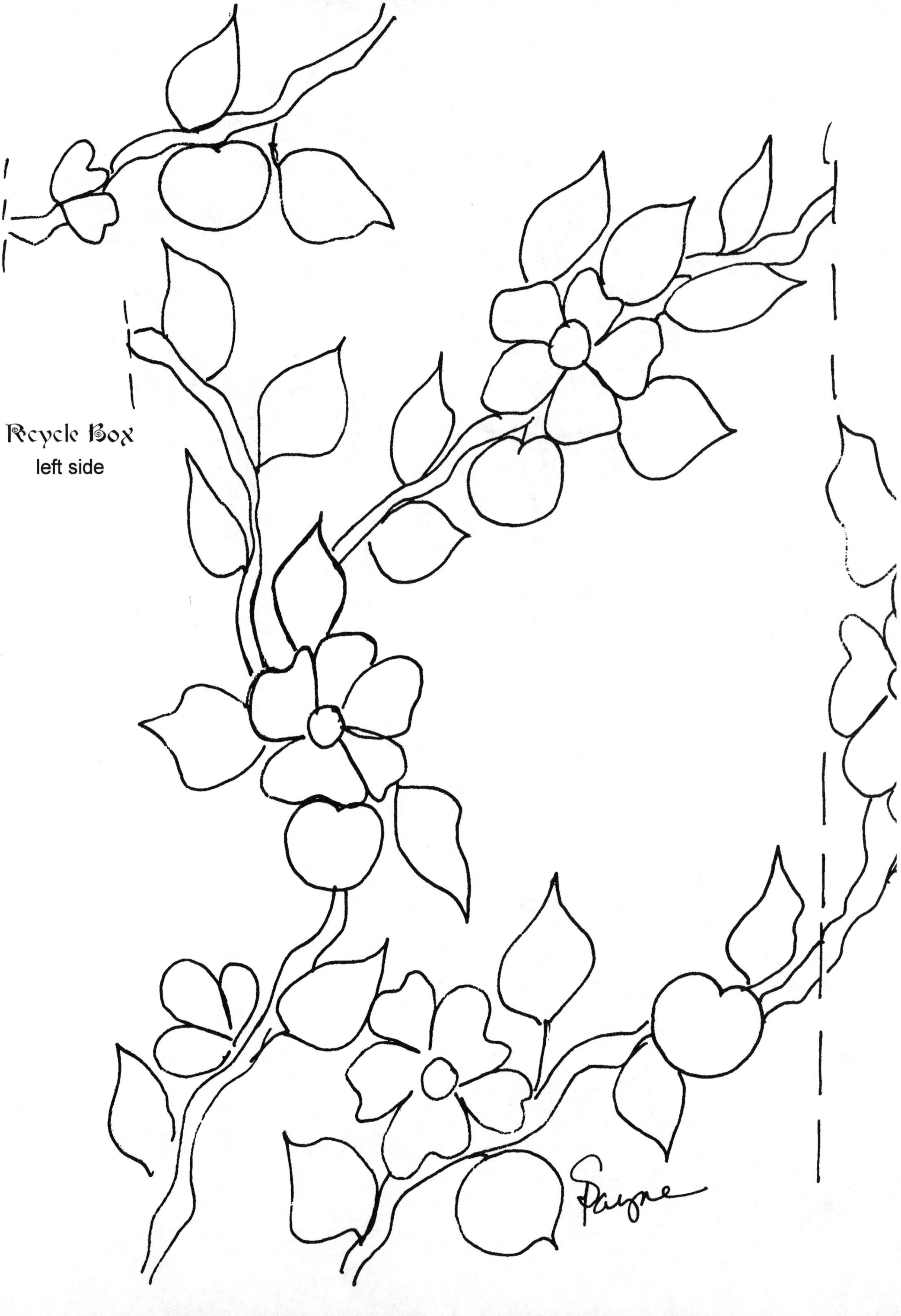

Payne

BasKet

color photo on page 27

Palette

Black Cherry	Light Ivory
Rose Petal Pink	Magnolia White
English Yew Green	Sea Green
Village Green	Dizzel Grey
Sweetheart Blush	Payne's Grey
Butter Yellow	

Delta Crackle
Renaissance Foil - Mother of Pearl Kit

BASKET

1. Apply two coats of Black Cherry to the outside surface of the basket.
2. Apply two coats of Light ivory to the inside, outside band and the bottom of the basket.
3. Let dry between coats.

Hint clean the studs with a cotton tip soaked in Delta brush cleaner.

4. Apply one coat of crackle to the Black Cherry areas
.

Hint: when applying crackle brush only enough to eliminate drips. Do not over brush, you are laying on the crackle rather than brushing out. Brush in one direction and let dry.

5. Apply one coat of Light Ivory over the crackle. Use enough paint and brush in one direction only. Brush only to eliminate drips and do not over brush.
6. Cracks should appear shortly after the Light Ivory has been applied. Let dry.

Background

1. Shade all the fence posts, band and the edge of the handle with Dizzle Grey

2. Sponge Village Green around the bottom, keep it light and airy.
3. Sponge Sea Green around the bottom.
4. Pull stems with Sea Green.
5. Stipple the stems with Black Cherry and highlight with Magnolia White.
6. Paint small five stroke flowers around the bottom with Rose Petal Pink.
7. Shade with Sweetheart Blush and highlight with Magnolia White.
8. Paint in centers with Butter Yellow and highlight with Magnolia White.
9. Double load a round brush with Village Green and Sea Green and pull leaves around the flowers.

DRAGON FLIES

1. Paint the bugs with Payne's Grey
2. Highlight the bodies with Light ivory.

BEE

1. Paint the body Butter yellow, let dry. Paint stripes with Payne's Grey.
2. Glue body to the wings

WINGS

1. Apply adhesive to the wings, let dry.
2. Press on Mother of Pearl foil and lift up.

LADY BUG

1. Paint with Black Cherry, let dry. Add dots with Payne's Grey.
2. Glue bug onto the basket handle.

Finishing

As described in the front of the book.

BasKet

repeat pattern to go around box

Placemats

color photo on page 27

Palette

Lavender Lace

Light Ivory

Rose Cloud

English Yew Green

White

Butter Yellow

Autumn Brown

Black Cherry

Rose Petal Pink

Light Ivory

Village Green

Payne's Grey

Navy Blue

PLACEMATS

1. Base coat in Navy Blue. Let dry.
2. Sponge on Lavender Lace and Light Ivory. Let dry.
3. Trace on the patterns.
4. Base coat the ribbon in Rose Petal Pink.
5. Shade with Rose Cloud and highlight with White.
6. Shade darker areas with Black Cherry.
7. Re-enforce the light areas with White.
8. Add a ruffle to the ribbon with White.
9. Base coat the leaves with Green Sea.
10. Shade with English Yew Green.
11. Highlight with Village Green.
12. Veins are put in with Village Green.

White flowers

1. Base coat with White.
2. Shade with Lavender Lace.
3. Highlight with White.
4. Shade darker areas with Payne's Grey
5. Flower centers are stippled in with Butter Yellow and shaded with Autumn Brown.
6. Highlight with White.
7. Dot in centers with Payne's Grey and White.

Pink flowers

1. Base coat with Rose Petal Pink.
2. Shade with Rose Cloud
3. Highlight with Light Ivory
4. Shade dark areas with Black Cherry
5. Re-enforce the light areas with White.
6. Tip the leaves of the pink flowers with Black Cherry and the white flowers with Rose Cloud.

Pansy centers

With a liner, make two comma strokes in White and add a dot of Butter Yellow to the center.

Finishing

Around the edge draw in the border with the gold pen.

Finish as described in the front of the book.

Daisy Placemat

Pansy Placemat

Pink Blossom Placemat
right side of pattern on page 29

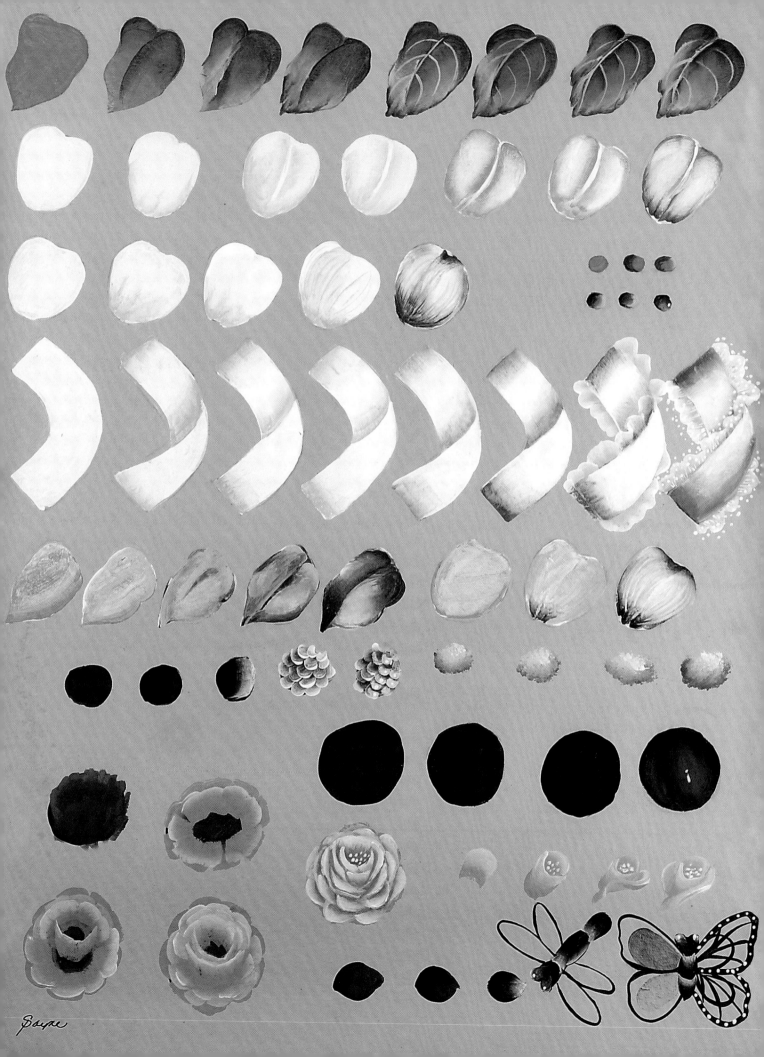

Sayre

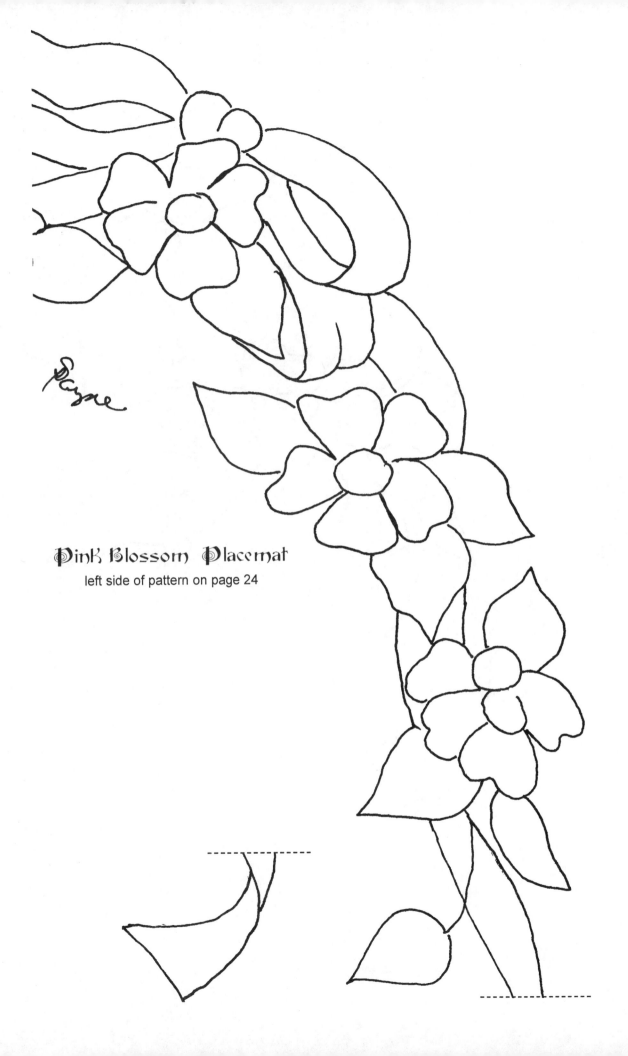

Pink Blossom Placemat

left side of pattern on page 24

White Blossom Placemat

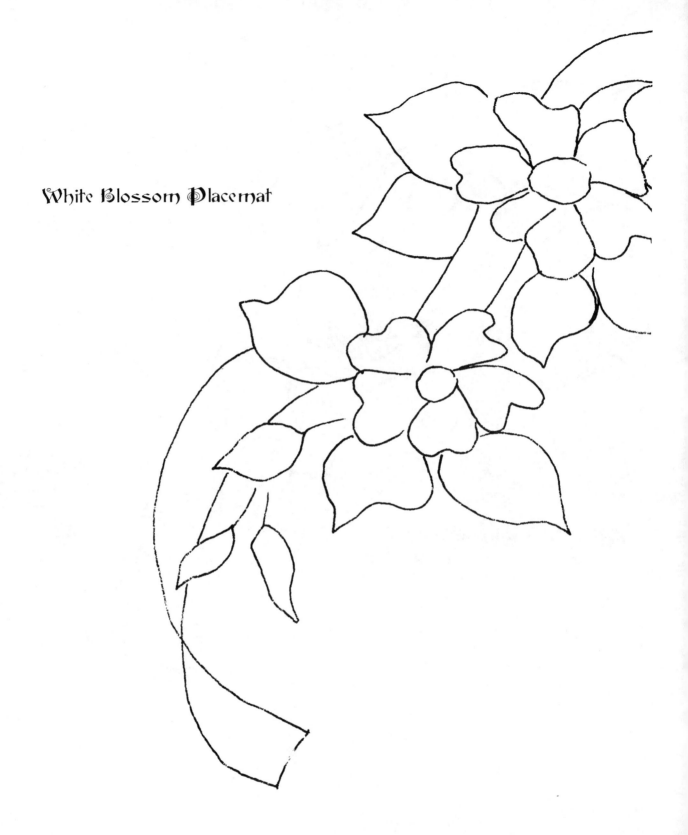

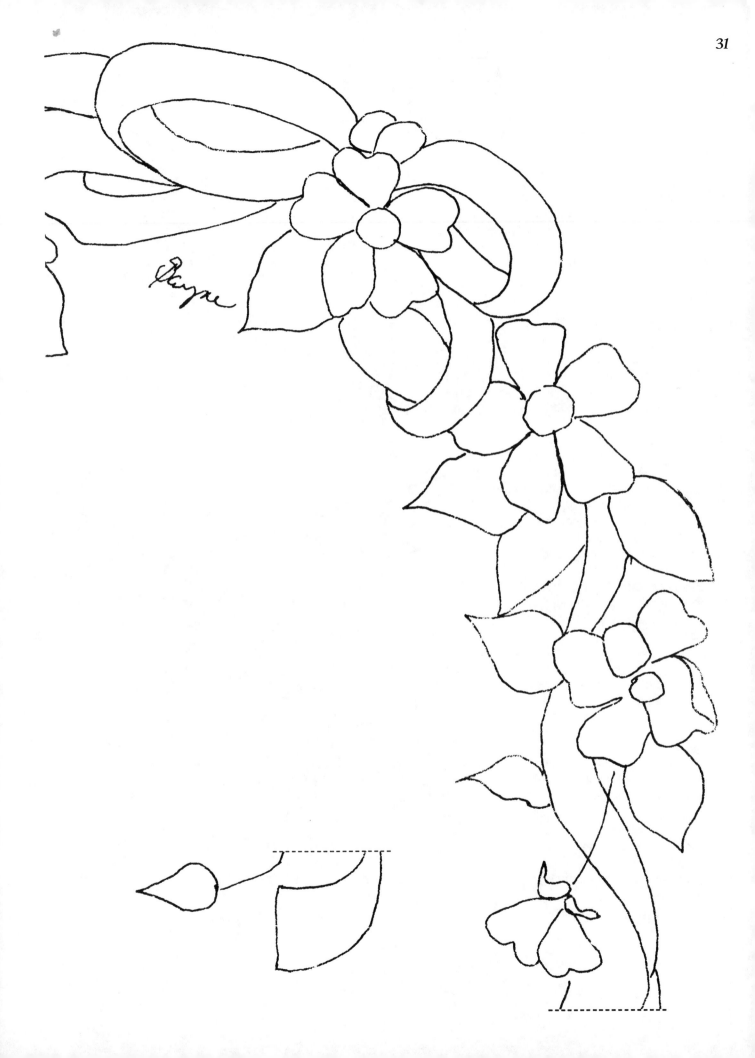

Tulip Tray

color photo on page 28

Palette

Magnolia White	Rose Cloud
Chocolate Cherry	Rose Petal Pink
Sweet heart Blush	Light Ivory
Sea Green	English Yew Green
Village Green	Mallard Green
Charcoal	Chambray Blue
White	
Gold Leaf	

TULIP TRAY

1. Apply a coat of Magnolia White to the front of the tray.
2. Paint the back with two coats of Rose Cloud
3. Paint around the front edge with Chocolate Cherry.
4. Wet the background with a damp sponge, then sponge on Magnolia White, Rose Petal Pink and Rose Cloud. Blend colors to a soft transition
5. Add vein lines of Magnolia White and Sweetheart Blush. Sponge into the background.
6. Trace on the pattern.
7. Base coat the tulips, the ribbon and the dogwood with Light Ivory, the leaves with Green Sea.

Leaves

1. Shade the leaves with English Yew Green.
2. Highlight with Village Green.
3. Put in the vein lines with Village Green.
4. Pick out several leaves and wash them with Mallard Green to add variety to the leaves.
5. Side load an angle shader with Charcoal and shade the extremely dark areas.
6. Side load with Village Green and re-enforce the extremely light areas.
7. Tip the edges with Sweetheart Blush.

Dogwood

1. Shade petals with Village Green.
2. Add vein lines with Village Green
3. Highlight with Magnolia White.
4. Shade dark areas with Chambray Blue
5. Re-enforce light areas with White
6. Tip ends with Sweetheart Blush
7. Shade dark areas with Sweetheart Blush

Dogwood Centers
1. Base coat the centers with Sea Green.
2. Shade with English Yew Green
3. Highlight with Village Green and add a sparkle with White.

Tulips
1. Add vein lines with Magnolia White.
2. Shade with Village Green.
3. 2 nd shading is with Rose Cloud
4. Highlight with Magnolia White
5. Add deeper shading to the petals with Sweetheart Blush.

Ribbon
1. Shade with Chambray Blue
2. Highlight with White
3. 2nd shading is with Chambray Blue and Chocolate Cherry mix.
4. Using the glue pen draw in the lines on the ribbon.
5. When dry press on gold leaf.

Ruffles
1. Side load the angle shader with White.
2. With the heel of the brush next to the ribbon wiggle on the ruffle. Pay attention to the way the ribbon turns.

Finishing
1. Draw a line around the edge of the tray with the glue pen. Let dry and press on gold leaf.
2. Paint the edge of the tray with adhesive and let dry.
3. Press on gold leaf and wipe off excess.

Frosted Plate

color photo on page 28

Palette

Cherry	Rose Cloud
Magnolia White	English Yew Green
Village Green	Green Sea
Chambray Blue	Charcoal
Mallard Green	Sweet heart Blush
White	Payne's Grey

Gold leaf

FROSTED PLATE
1. Transfer the design to the plate.
2. Base coat the leaves with Green Sea, the ribbon and the dogwood with Magnolia White, the plums and berries with Black Cherry.

Leaves
1. Shade with English Yew Green.
2. Highlight with Village Green.
3. Put in the vein lines with Village Green.
4. Pick out several leaves and wash them with Mallard Green to add variety to the leaves.
5. Side load an angle shader with Charcoal and shade the extremely dark areas.
6. Side load with Village Green and re-enforce the extremely light areas.
7. Tip the edges with Sweetheart Blush.

Dogwood
1. Shade petals with Village Green.
2. Add vein lines with Village Green
3. Highlight with Magnolia White.
4. Shade dark areas with Chambray Blue
5. Re-enforce light areas with White.
6. Tip ends with Sweetheart Blush
7. Shade dark areas with Sweetheart Blush

Dogwood Centers
1. Base coat with Green Sea
2. Shade with English Yew Green
3. Highlight with Village Green and add a sparkle with White.

Ribbon
1. Shade with Rose Cloud
2. Highlight with White
3. 2nd shading is with Rose Blush

Plums
1. Highlight with Sweetheart Blush
2. Shade with Chocolate Cherry
3. Shade the darker areas with Payne's Grey
4. Reinforce highlights with a mix of 2 Sweetheart Blush and 1 Magnolia White Berries.

Berries
1. Highlight with Sweetheart Blush
2. Shade with Payne's Grey
3. Side load an angle shader with Magnolia White and paint in the seedpods
4. Highlight some of the seedpods with White.

Finishing
1. Apply two coats of Satin glaze to painted area only.

36

Fruit and Flowers
Fabric Skirt
color photo on page 28

Palette
Delta fabric paint:

White
Violet
Leather
Wild Berry
Lavender

Deep Clover Pink
English Yew
Egg Yolk
Leaf Green

Freezer paper
Heat transfer pencil
Battenburg Lace table skirt
Iron
Pressing cloth
Delta Textile Medium

Instructions

1. Trace the pattern onto tracing paper.
2. Turn the tracing over and retrace the design using a heat transfer pencil (red)
3. Position the pattern (red side down) over the cloth and using a pressing cloth iron to transfer the design. The design will transfer several times before it has to be traced again. Four repeats were used on this skirt.
4. Iron the freezer paper to the under side of the skirt to prevent the paint from leaking through. Shiny side will stick to the fabric.

The fabric medium will be used as a means of moving the paint in this technique. It is therefore very important to apply medium to each pattern piece before it is painted. The medium needs to cover the entire shape before any color is applied. However, don't use an excessive amount to accomplish this. I would suggest you have a separate small clean brush to use for applying medium only.

Ribbon

1. Cover one section of the ribbon with fabric medium. Wipe out the brush.
2. Side load into Lavender and apply to the darkest areas indicated. Wipe the brush and pull color out to cover desired area. Repeat to paint the entire ribbon.
3. Side load into Violet and apply to the darkest areas. Wipe your brush and pull color out to cover desired area.
4. Side load into White and apply to the lightest areas. Wipe your brush and pull color out to cover desired area.
5. Thin Violet with fabric medium and using a liner brush draw in outlines.
6. Side load into Lavender and paint on the ruffles. Ruffles are made using side loaded brush and wiggle strokes along the length of the ribbon. They are not undercoated with fabric medium and are applied quickly.
7. Reapply Violet to the darkest areas of the ribbon.

Flowers:

1. Apply fabric medium to the petal. Wipe out brush.
2. Side load the brush in Pink and apply color to the darkest areas of the petal. Wipe off

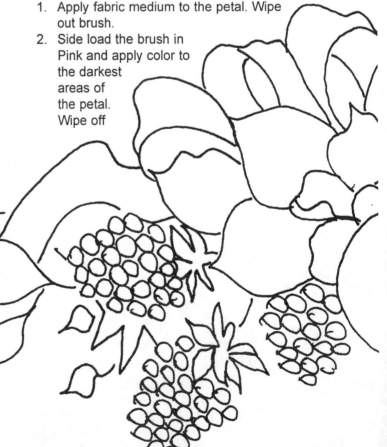

brush and pull out the color covering the desired area.

3. Side load into White and apply to the light areas. Wipe brush and pull out color to cover desired area.
4. Side load into Wild Berry and apply to the darkest areas. Wipe and pull out color.
5. Side load with Wild Berry and apply around the flower center. Repeat filling in all flower petals.
6. Add tints of Violet to some of the petals.

Flower centers
7. Apply fabric medium to the center.
8. Stipple center with Egg Yolk. Wipe out brush.
9. Pick up Leather and stipple bottom edge.
10. Wipe out brush and pick up white. Stipple the light center.

Leaves
1. Apply a coat of fabric medium to the leaf. Side load into Leaf Green and apply to the dark area. Wipe brush and pull out color to cover desired area.
2. Repeat with all leaves.
3. Darken some of the leaves with English Yew and some with Deep Clover.
4. Wipe out the brush and pull color to desired areas.
5. Add tints of Pink to some of the leaves.
6. Thin English Yew with fabric medium and add the veins, stems and lines around the leaves.

Fruit
1. Apply a coat of fabric medium to the fruit.
2. Side load into Wild Berry and apply to the darkest area. Wipe brush
3. Pull out color to desired areas.
4. Side load into Violet and apply to the darkest area. Wipe brush
5. Pull out color to desired areas.
6. Side load into White and apply to the lightest areas. Wipe brush and pull color to cover desired areas.
7. Side load into Violet and apply to darkest areas.
8. Thin white with fabric medium and apply the "smile" highlight to the fruit.

Berries
1. Apply a coat of fabric medium to the berry.
2. Side load into Pink and apply to the darkest area. Wipe brush and pull color to cover desired areas.
3. Side load into Violet and apply to the darkest areas. Wipe brush and pull color to cover desired area.
4. Side load into white and paint in the berry cells as shown. Let dry.

Garment may now be heat set by ironing and put on your pretty table and used. Thanks for painting with me. Sherry

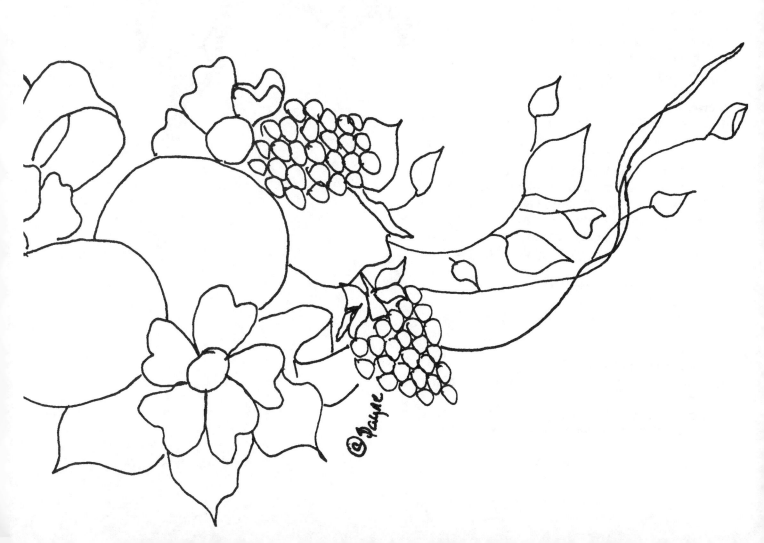

 # Popcorn Box
color photo on inside back cover

Palette

Magnolia White	Violet Pearl
Pinkie Pearl	Purple
Dusty Plumb	Payne's Grey
Green Sea	Village Green
English Yew Green	Magnolia White
White	Rose Petal Pink
Tape	

Instructions

1. Base coat the box in Magnolia White and the top and bottom in English Yew Green.
2. Smoke the box
3. Tape off the box in a x pattern
4. Shade all the remaining area with English Yew Green.
5. Pull off tape and shade the cross pieces. (don't worry if you get confused, I did, it really doesn't show when it is finished.)
6. Trace on pattern.

Leaves

1. Base coat with Green Sea
2. Shade with English Yew Green
3. Highlight with Village Green
4. Tip with Purple
5. Veins are put in with Village Green

Flowers

1. Load with Dusty Plumb and tip into Rose Petal Pink. Run your brush back and forth on the palette to get a nice blending of color.
2. Starting with the back petals paint in the roses. With each petal pick up more and more Rose Petal Pink. Blend the color on the brush before you paint each petal. Paint the rose petal by petal not row by row. The petals should get lighter as they come forward.
3. When the rose is complete go back and shade with Purple
4. Highlight with Magnolia White.
5. Add dots to the center with White.
6. Squiggles are painted in with English Yew Green.

Butterfly

1. Base coat with Paynes Grey.
2. Highlight bottom with Violet Pearl and the top with Pinkie Pearl
3. Add dots and shade the body with White
4. Glue onto the front and top of the box.

Finish as directed in the front of the book.

Detail of Butterfly

Popcorn Box
Back Side

Popcorn Box
left side

Popcorn Box
Right Side

Payne

Sign Board
color photo on inside back cover

Palette

Chocolate Cherry
Rose Cloud
Magnolia White
Green Sea
Chambray Blue
Dizzle Grey
Mallard Green
Payne's Grey
Dusty Plumb
Aqua Cool Pearl

Rose Petal Pink
Wild Rose
English Yew Green
Village Green
Charcoal
Sweetheart Blush
White
Navy Blue
Baby Blue Pearl

Monogram Magic Stencils
Tape

SIGN BOARD

1. Base coat the inside of the board with two coats of Chocolate Cherry.
2. Base coat the edge with two coats of Magnolia White.
3. Smoke the edge of the signboard.
4. Trace on the pattern.

Ribbon

1. Base coat the ribbon with Rose Petal Pink
2. Shade with Drizzle Grey
3. Highlight with Magnolia White
4. 2nd shading to the ribbon is with Chambray Blue.
5. Mix Chambray Blue with Chocolate Cherry and shade the extremely dark areas of the ribbon. (two parts CB one part CC)
6. Highlight with White.

The Leaves

1. Base coat the leaves with Green Sea
2. Shade with English Yew Green.
3. Highlight with Village Green.
4. Tip the leaves with Sweetheart Blush.
5. Put in the vein lines with Village Green.
6. Pick out several leaves and wash them with Mallard Green to add variety to the leaves.
7. Side load with Charcoal and shade the extremely dark areas.
8. Side load with Village Green and re-enforce the extremely light areas.

Dogwood

1. Shade petals with Village Green.
2. Add vein lines with Village Green
3. Highlight with Magnolia White.
4. Shade dark areas with Chambray Blue
5. Re-enforce light areas with White
6. Tip ends with Sweetheart Blush
7. Shade dark areas with Sweetheart Blush

Dogwood Centers

1. Base coat the centers with Green Sea.
2. Shade with English Yew Green
3. Highlight with Village Green and add a sparkle with White.

Roses

1. Load with Dusty Plumb and tip into Rose Petal Pink. Run your brush back and forth on the palette to get a nice blending of color.
2. Starting with the back petals paint in the roses. With each petal pick up more and more Rose Petal Pink. Blend the color on the brush before you paint each petal. Paint the rose petal by petal not row by row. The petals should get lighter as they come forward.
3. When the rose is complete go back and shade with Wild Rose
4. 2nd shading-Shade extremely dark areas with Sweetheart Blush.
5. Highlight with Magnolia White.
6. The extremely light areas are reinforced with White
7. Add dots to the center with Magnolia White.

Tulips

1. Base coat the tulips with Magnolia White.
2. Add vein lines with Magnolia White.
3. Shade veins with Village Green
4. Shade the tulips with Rose Cloud
5. Highlight the tulips with White
6. Add deeper shading to the petals with Chocolate Cherry.

Numbers

1. Using Delta's Monogram Magic Stencils, position numbers on the board as desired.
2. With a small sponge, sponge the numbers with Magnolia White. Let dry and remove stencils.

Butterfly

1. Base coat the butterfly with Navy Blue
2. Shade the top of the wings with Baby Blue Pearl
3. Shade the bottom of the wings with Aqua Cool Pearl
4. With a liner paint in the lines with Payne's Grey
5. Add dots with Magnolia White.
6. Glue onto the signboard.

Finishing

1. Apply two coats of varnish or glaze of your choice.
2. Sand surface and wipe off.
3. Apply one more coat of varnish or glaze.
4. Wax with bee's wax.

1

Wind Chimes

color photo on inside back cover

Palette

English Yew Green   Black Cherry
Butter Yellow   Green Sea
Village Green   Payne's Grey
Violet Pearl   Pinkie Pearl
White

Three small wood leaves and a butterfly cut out

Instructions

1. Base coat the chimes in Black Cherry.
2. Trace on the pattern.
3. Base coat the leaves in Green Sea.
4. Shade with English Yew Green.
5. Highlight with Village Green.
6. Add accents with Butter Yellow and Black Cherry
7. The outline work is done with the gold leaf pen.
8. Follow the same leaf instructions for the 3 small wooden leaves.

Butterfly

1. Base coat in Payne's Grey
2. Shade the top half in Violet Pearl
3. Shade the bottom half with Pinkie Pearl.
4. Outline the wings with Payne's Grey
5. Add White dots with a stylus.

Wind Chime
patterns

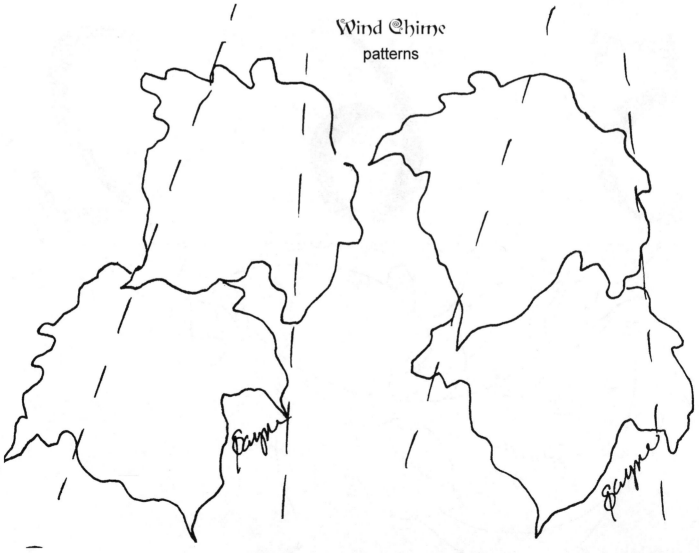

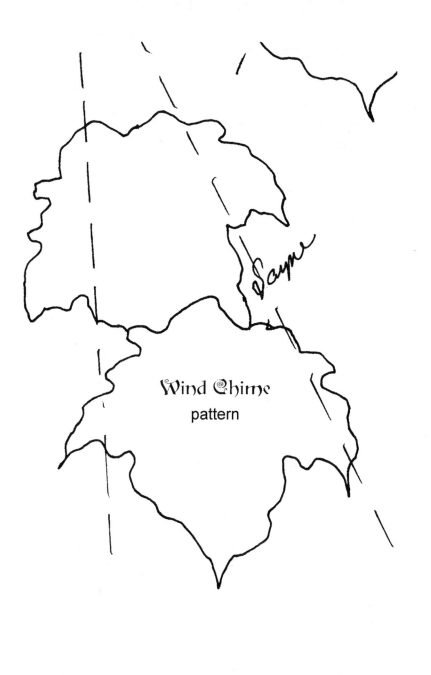

Wind Chime
pattern

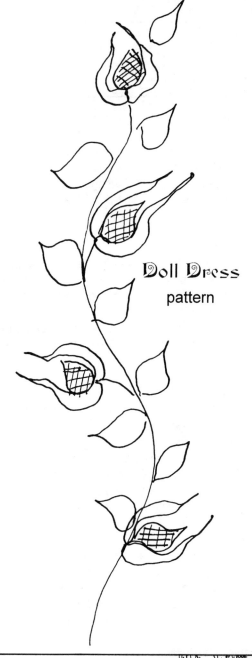

Doll Dress
pattern

Doll
color photo on back

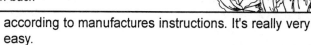

Use the Doll kit, Heirlooms from the Heart 18" doll, from Bell Ceramic. This comes complete with eyes and hair.

It is already painted and easy to assemble. Clothes and other items may be purchased separately or sewn by hand.

Palette

Rose Cloud	White
English Yew Green	Village Green

Instructions

Assemble the doll and buy or make the clothes according to manufactures instructions. It's really very easy.

Flowers

1. Flowers are base coated with Rose Cloud.

2. Highlight with White on the tips.

3. Leaves are done with a double loaded brush of Village Green and English Yew Green. Press down and pull up.

4. The line work and stems are done with a dirty Green brush.

48

Noel
color photo on back cover

Palette
Lavender Lace	Black Cherry
Light Ivory	Rose Cloud
Magnolia White	English Yew Green
Green Sea	Village Green
Butter Yellow	Navy Blue
Kim Gold	

Instructions
1. Base coat the candles in Magnolia White.
2. Smoke the surface.
3. Apply two coats of Kim Gold to the tops.
4. Trace on the pattern.
5. Base coat the ribbon in Lavender Lace, the flower centers and leaves in Sea Green and the flowers in Rose Cloud.

Ribbon
1. Shade the ribbon with a mix of two parts Lavender Lace and one part Navy Blue
2. Highlight the ribbon with Light Ivory.
3. Dark areas of the ribbon are shaded with Navy Blue.
4. Reinforce the highlight with White.
5. Draw scallops along the ribbon with Kim Gold and put on dots with a stylus.

Leaves
1. Shade with English Yew Green.
2. Highlight with Village Green.
3. Add accents of Butter Yellow and White.
4. Tip the leaves with Black Cherry.
5. Vein lines are put in with Village Green.

Flower Centers
1. Shade with English Yew Green.
2. Highlight with Village Green.
3. Add accents of White and Butter Yellow.
4. The stamens are painted with a liner brush and Black Cherry.

Flowers
1. Shade with Village Green.
2. Second shading is done with Black Cherry.
3. Highlight with White.
4. Add accents of Butter Yellow.
5. Vein lines are put in with Village Green.

Letters
1. You can free hand letters or use Delta's Monogram Magic Letters.
2. Apply two coats of Kim Gold to the letters. Let dry between coats.

Finish as described in the front of the book.

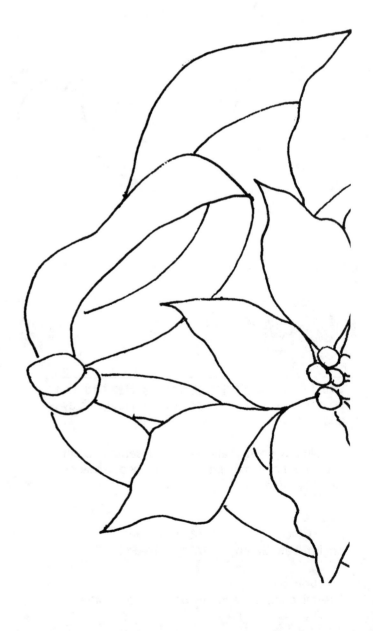

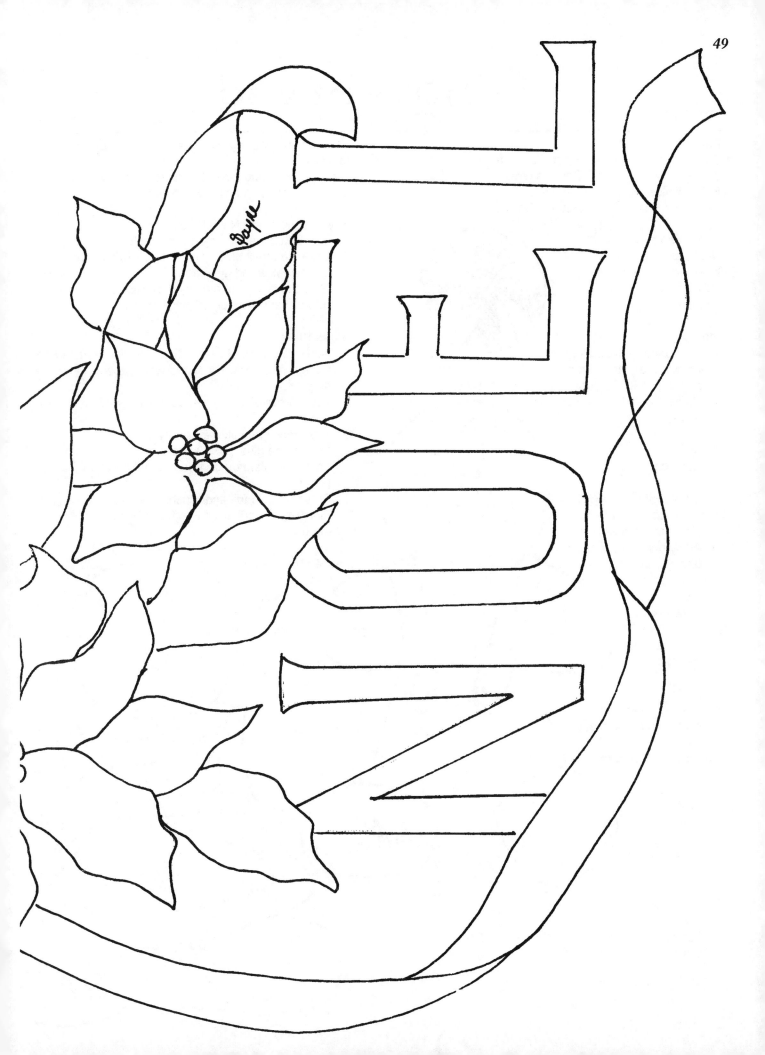

Gingerbread
color photo on back cover

Palette
Black Cherry
White
Butter Yellow
Fleshtone Base

Magnolia White
Payne's Grey
Navy Blue
Autumn Brown

Saran Wrap
Gold Leaf
Wood circles and stars
Liquid nails

Plate
1. Base coat in Magnolia White.
2. Smoke the plate surface.
3. Apply glue to the edge of the plate. Let dry.
4. Press on gold foil and brush off extra.

Stars
1. Base coat with Fleshtone base.
2. Shade with Butter Yellow
3. Apply colored dots to simulate sprinkles.
4. Apply one coat of sparkle glaze.

Candy
1. Base coat with White.
2. Paint stripes with Black Cherry. Two coats.
3. Glue stars and candy circles on to the plate.

Gingerbread people
1. Base coat in Fleshtone Base.
2. Shade around the edges with Autumn Brown.
3. Draw squiggle lines with White.
4. Trace on pattern
5. Paint in eyes and mouth with Payne's Grey
6. Cheeks are floated in with Black Cherry

Clothes are painted with a side loaded brush as follows:
Girl - Dress and bow are painted with Black Cherry. Apron and collar are White.

Boy - Shorts are Navy Blue
Buttons are painted with White
7. Glue the small balsa wood pieces to the backs of the ginger bread girls feet
8. Glue the boys and girls by their hands and feet. Use rubber bands to hold in place till dry.

Glass Plate
1. Apply one coat of Black Cherry to the surface of the frosted plate. While paint is wet proceed to the next step.
2. Lay a piece of scrunched up Saran Wrap on top of the wet paint.
3. Push down and lift off. Let dry.
4. Pour some glue into a saucer
5. Stand the plate up on end and pull through the glue. Let dry
6. Press on gold foil and brush off extra.
7. Finish as described in the front of the book.

Assemble all parts and place a pillar candle in the middle of the kids.